The Personality of a Libra Explained

Author:

Sikandar Sami

+92-300-8016343

Libra (September 23 - October 22)

Libra is an air sign spoke to by the scales (strikingly, the main lifeless thing of the zodiac), an affiliation that mirrors Libra's obsession with parity and concordance. Libra is fixated on evenness and endeavors to make balance in all everyday issues. These air signs are the people of good taste of the zodiac: Ruled by Venus, the planet that administers love, excellence, and cash, Libras venerate high craftsmanship, intellectualism, and connoisseurship. Smooth Libras need to encircle themselves with staggering items and make conditions that mirror their lovely tastes. As needs be, these air signs make phenomenal architects, decorators, workmanship pundits, and beauticians.

While Libra's contrary sign, Aries, speaks to "me," Libra represents "we." Relationships are vital for Libras, who discover balance in friendship. They love amicable associations with popular mates, particularly the individuals who make alluring eye candy. (Libra administers the skin, and these air signs are profoundly energetic by physical appearances. It is highly unlikely Libra would prefer to unwind than with a sumptuous face veil.)

Libras are normally coupled, and when they will be, they should be cautious about looking for consideration outside the tons of their connections. Since they attempt to keep everybody cheerful and drew in, they may wind up enticed to push the restrictions of their concurrences with their accomplices. Human satisfying Libras must recall that the joy of their friends and family and the wellbeing of their connections is a higher priority than keeping up the consideration of far off admirers.

Libra is a cardinal sign, which implies Libras are likewise incredible at propelling new activities. Since Libras think about numerous viewpoints in all interests, be that as it may, these air signs battle with hesitation. Rather than continually looking for outside viewpoints, Libras would do well to create (and trust) their own instinct. Their trademark irresoluteness aside, Libras can explore basically any social circumstance, easily settling clashes by essentially turning on the appeal.

Book: The Personality of a Libra, Explained - Author: Sikandar Sami

Contents

LIBRA ZODIAC SIGN LIBRA HOROSCOPE

Component: Air

Quality: Cardinal

Shading: Pink, Green

Day: Friday

Ruler: Venus

Most noteworthy Overall Compatibility: Aries, Sagittarius

Fortunate Numbers: 4, 6, 13, 15, 24

Date extend: September 23 - October 22

Libra (September 23 - October 22)

Book: The Personality of a Libra, Explained - Author: Sikandar Sami

LIBRA TRAITS

Qualities: Cooperative,diplomatic, generous, impartial, social

Shortcomings: Indecisive, maintains a strategic distance from showdowns, will convey resentment, self indulgence

Libra likes: Harmony, delicacy, imparting to other people, the outside

Libra loathes: Violence, foul play, windbags, similarity

Individuals brought into the world under the indication of Libra are serene, reasonable, and they scorn being distant from everyone else. Organization is significant for them, as their mirror and somebody enabling them to be simply the mirror. These people are entranced by equalization and balance, they are in a steady pursue for equity and fairness, acknowledging through life that the main thing that ought to be genuinely imperative to themselves in their own internal center of character. This is somebody prepared to do about anything to dodge strife, keeping the harmony at whatever point conceivable

The indication of Libra is an Air sign, set among Gemini and Aquarius, giving these people steady mental improvements, solid keenness and a sharp psyche. They will be motivated by acceptable books, outlandish conversations and individuals who have a ton to state. Every Libra agent must be cautious when conversing with others, for when they are compelled to choose about something that is coming their direction, or to pick sides, they abruptly understand that they may be in an inappropriate spot and encircled by wrong individuals. No accomplice should cause them to overlook that they have their own feeling.

Planet administering the indication of Libra is Venus, making these individuals extraordinary darlings yet in addition enamored with costly, material things. Their lives should be advanced by music, workmanship, and excellent spots they get an opportunity to visit.

7

Libra – The Measure of Our Souls The most brief fantasy of all appears to introduce a decent relationship to the most limited star grouping in the sky, you may even say that it is non-existent, introduced by the pincers of Scorpio. Libra is one speck of parity in the ocean of various limits, showed uniquely through the fifteenth level of this glorious sign, an item among creatures and individuals. There is something terribly shaky about Libra, as though they were uncertain which plate to trouble straightaway, mindful that things pass and instruct us to be cautious around others. Whatever we do in the course of our lives, just serves to point the path for our Souls towards that "higher force" to at long last measure our reality. Revealing to us where we turned out badly or what we did well, Libras unwittingly instruct us that genuine freedom stows away in delicacy.

LBRA LOVE AND SEX

Finding a viable accomplice will be the principle need in the life of individuals brought into the world with their Sun in Libra. When they start a sentimental relationship, keeping up harmony and amicability become the most significant thing and their essential objective. Their enchanting character and their devotion to every relationship makes their similarity with others fulfilling, yet that fallen Sun they experience to mend frequently makes difficulty in their passionate world.

Libra is the indication of marriage, making its agents open for conventional pathways of adoration. Despite the fact that the component of Air gives them a great deal of adaptability, they will in any case feel the solid draw towards convention and their wants will in the end go to cherish put in writing, efficient and filling a need to make a specific picture for the external world. As it were, every Libra is looking for an accomplice who can define clear limits, as though hoping to be secured by them yet without their pride being jeopardized simultaneously.

This is a sign profoundly associated with sexuality for Scorpio rises where it closes. They look for profound, significant relationship and despite the fact that they don't experience difficulty relating with individuals they aren't generally near, the main genuine fulfillment in their adoration life originates from complete acquiescence of body and soul. It is the gravity of Libra to impart as long as they can remember to somebody, with a test to be autonomous and mindful of their center character simultaneously.

At the point when a Libra has decided on being with somebody, they have just picked well, yet it will assist with recognizing what holds them up of accomplishing joy or pushes them advances coordinating sings in gadgets beneath:

LIBRA FRIENDS AND FAMILY

Companions – Libra delegates are exceptionally social and placed their companions in the spotlight, yet now and again raise their desire bars excessively high, and pick kinships that cause them to feel better than the individual remaining before them. Their temperament makes them uncertain which is the reason they may show an absence of. In any case, this won't make them any less put resources into their connections when another person takes the implement and shows enthusiasm for them. Thoughtful and quiet, they can convey through any issue on the off chance that they need to, and will frequently help other people comprehend the opposite side of their own contentions and issue with others.

Family – Born into a family that gave them a specific shortcoming of the Sun, Libra can regularly move blame between relatives without monitoring doing as such. In consistent quest for concordance these people tend to concur with their folks and kin just to dodge strife, being the one to pull back when a test comes their direction. They have to support their character and regularly go to isolation just to find their own perspective among many. On the off chance that they are all around assembled and chipped away at their inward feeling of intensity, they find ease in being a decent parent and good example, prepared to share all that they know with their youngsters.

LIBRA CAREER AND MONEY

For every Libra, the way in to a cheerful life is in a fine equalization, which means they won't resolve to work without separating enough an ideal opportunity for their private life and their friends and family, and in the event that they do, they will feel like they have to liberate from it. They can be cherished pioneers despite the fact that they now and then come up short on the activity expected to sort out individuals who work for them, and will endeavor to merit benefits that come their direction. In look for truth and equity, they are acceptable attorneys and judges, and can likewise be effective as ambassadors, planners and writers on the off chance that they have sustained their imaginative side from adolescence. They will function admirably in a gathering, and can be persuading and talented speakers.

Money related part of their lives is regularly leveled out, which likely wouldn't be the situation in the event that they had a simpler time choosing what they need to purchase. When they begin scrutinizing their budgetary decisions, odds are they won't go through any cash whatsoever, just on the grounds that it was difficult to settle on a choice of any sort. They balance among sparing and spending really well and despite the fact that they appreciate style and fine garments, they infrequently let their wants for spending outwit them.

Step by step instructions to ATTRACT THE LIBRA MAN

Libra men value all that is excellent and look for an accomplice to motivate them with their appearance. This may sound shallow, yet the truth of the matter is they need mental and visual boosts to settle on choice cycles simpler and drive them into a genuine relationship in the first place. When they have chosen to be with somebody, they generally make genuine, long haul bonds, suffering easily through the tough situations realizing they have just settled on the ideal decision in any case. A Libra man needs to examine everything with his accomplice, from day by day matters to huge shared undertakings throughout everyday life.

This is a man in look for a join forces with quality of will and certainty, somebody to direct the way when he feels lost or uncertain. When he finds the ideal individual, he will effectively fulfill them, turning their consideration exclusively to their accomplice and regularly overlooking himself simultaneously. This man is profoundly sentimental in his center and in look for genuine affection to last him a lifetime.

Book: The Personality of a Libra, Explained - Author: Sikandar Sami

To tempt a Libra lady one must be a decent conversationalist and audience. She appreciates being instructed about new things and appreciates discussing herself and her own advantages, the same amount of as she loves sinking profound into her accomplice's life. She is enchanting, astute, and discovers answers for issues that emerge en route effortlessly. Her accomplice needs to cause her intrigued and to remain alert from the outset, making her inquiry her own drive and decisions, while likewise direct and amazing enough.

Being governed by Venus a Libra lady has a characteristic propensity to have certain emotional episodes, yet this won't make her any less just in her manners. When she experiences passionate feelings and offers a home with an accomplice, she will deal with them, make them look great, and keep their public activity sorted out and balanced to accepted practices they live in.

Viable Signs Libra Should Consider: Gemini, Leo, Sagittarius, Aquarius

The 10 Fundamental Libra Traits and the Best Advice for Libras

Libra is an air sign, and Libras are known for the love of being around others. Libras are unbelievably agreeable and honest, and are an indication that accepts solidly in the intensity of social association. Libras are probably the most intriguing and astute individuals around, and they have a ton to offer. Beneath, we'll talk about key Libra qualities, how Libras identify with others, and guidance for being a Libra and coexisting with the Libra in your life.

What Is a Libra?

A Libra is an individual conceived between September 23rd and October 22nd. Libras are known for being beguiling, delightful, and even. They blossom with making things organized and tastefully satisfying. They likewise want equalization, and they can be similarly as narcissistic as they are liberal.

Libras are additionally the rulers and sovereigns of bargain, and they like creation harmony between others. This makes them extraordinary pioneers, companions, and accomplices, and they can apply these positive characteristics to their own and expert lives.

Libra Personality Traits

Libras are energizing individuals to be near. Obviously, not all Libras are actually the equivalent, yet these key attributes of Libras are essential to know whether you are a Libra or need to find out about identifying with them.

Positive Libra Personality Traits

Probably the best Libra attributes are a feeling of decency and an active nature. They're important for why we love Libras.

Conciliatory

Libras are normal peacemakers and are specialists at being thoughtful and strategic in their connections and in gatherings. They pick their words cautiously and expect to discover shared view with however many individuals as would be prudent.

Book: The Personality of a Libra, Explained - Author: Sikandar Sami

Reasonable

Libras have a solid feeling of equity. They need to ensure everybody gets heard, and are energetic about ensuring that things are adjusted, particularly with regards to aggregate occasions.

Hopeful

Libras consistently like to look on the splendid side. They see the best in all individuals in all circumstances. They have extraordinary aims and think the best of individuals and thoughts. They generally have high trusts in beginning new undertakings and learning new things.

Social

There are not many signs more outgoing than Libras. Libras love being with individuals, and they love meeting new individuals, as well. They blossom with friendship, and they encircle themselves with intriguing individuals that can acquaint them with new things. Being social is one of the most central components of the Libra character.

Shrewd

Libras are clever, shrewd, and astounding conversationalists. They have dynamic minds and are sharp witted, which makes them extraordinary organization and incredible issue solvers.

Book: The Personality of a Libra, Explained - Author: Sikandar Sami

Pessimistic Libra Personality Traits

Libras are every one of the unique, and these "negative" Libra attributes are important for what makes them what their identity is. The negative Libra qualities are all aspect of their adoration for balance.

Uncertain

Libras' affection for equalization can impede them. They'll go through hours gauging the upsides and downsides of even the littlest choices. They need to satisfy everybody and experience difficulty focusing on something, regardless of whether it appears to be immaterial.

Non-Confrontational

Libras are peacemakers commonly. They are extraordinary at discovering bargain inside gatherings, regardless of whether it's between companions or in business settings, yet this implies they additionally experience difficulty confronting their issues and will put off troublesome conversations for as long as could be expected under the circumstances.

Self indulging

One of the defeats of the Libra is that they are somewhat self-ingested, so when things don't go completely directly for them, they feel like the world is finishing, and everybody is against them. They experience difficulty seeing the master plan in the midst of conflict, and rather center around themselves solely.

Book: The Personality of a Libra, Explained - Author: Sikandar Sami

Problematic

Libras are known for being unpredictable. While they are bunches of amusing to associate with, they are not generally the most dependable. Heaps of Libras are superb and steadfast companions, despite the fact that they may not appear at your supper anticipates time.

Vain

As we referenced, Libras love wonderful things, including themselves. You may discover a Libra taking selfies wherever they go, or investing heaps of energy in spoiling and appearances. They might be basic about how others look or be hesitant to spend time with individuals who they believe are less alluring.

Libra Traits in Relationships

We realize that the Libra character thrives in social settings. Find out about what Libras need in explicit connections is significant, since if Libras are by and large evident Libras, they're probably going to have heaps of connections to monitor.

Sentimental

One of the most famous Libra attributes is their affection for adoration. With their propensity to incline toward excellence and fervor, Libras get effectively love alcoholic. Nonetheless, while Libras will appreciate bunches of indulgences and appreciate the organization of sentimental accomplices, they're intense with regards to serious relationships. They pick cautiously with regards to life accomplices.

Non-romantic

You're practically ensured to make some incredible memories with a Libra. Notwithstanding being bunches of fun, Libras love to attempt new things and will help individuals in their lives become and remain receptive. They're devoted to ensuring individuals in their lives accomplish balance as well, and the Libra's cordial nature and optimism can come off on their loved ones.

Proficient

Authority easily falls into place for Libras, and as such they exceed expectations expertly when they're permitted to let their initiative abilities and inventiveness sparkle. Libras do best when taken off alone to create ventures. In any case, Libras don't have the best finish, so it's likewise imperative to ensure they're encircled by grounded individuals who are acceptable at taking bearing and completing things.

Guidance for Libras

#1: In your profession, ensure you're making new difficulties for yourself. As a Libra, you'll have to switch things up frequently, so to abstain from looking flaky you can channel that vitality into groundbreaking thoughts that advantage the entire gathering.

#2: Don't spare a moment to let your genuine nature show. Be the extraordinary and steadfast companion that you are, and don't sit around on individuals who judge you for your empathy and vision.

#3: You incline toward control when you're exhausted, so consistently attempt to take a look at yourself when you begin to feel eager. Channel that vitality into innovative activities or chipping in.

Book: The Personality of a Libra, Explained - Author: Sikandar Sami

#4: Be straightforward with yourself. Libras experience difficulty conceding their shortcomings. Try not to think about these things as negatives, only a piece of you that may require some additional consideration. Ensure you know where you have to improve, in light of the fact that else you may stroll over individuals without significance to, prompting some showdown.

#5: Speaking of encounter—address it smoothly and at an early stage. In the event that you do need to go up against somebody, ensure you have your calls attention to laid in advance and you stick to them in any event, when the discussion gets troublesome.

Tips for Relating to a Libra

#1: Compliments are everything to a Libra character. They're social butterflies, and giving outward indications of friendship will assist you with winning courtesy from the get-go in the relationship, and keep on helping keep the sparkle alive.

#2: Don't start ruckuses or be excessively basic toward a Libra. Libras maintain a strategic distance from showdown, so it's ideal to be open and forthright about things that are going on in the relationship and address a Libra as an equivalent.

#3: Let Libras take positions of authority. They're awesome at it, and don't be put off by a Libra concocting a thousand unique thoughts for bunch tasks or exercises. Assist them with picking one and stay grounded.

#4: Show that you thoroughly understand balance, as well. Libras need to adjust the scales regardless, and they need companions and accomplices that deal with them like equivalents and expertise to be ready and consistent in all parts of their lives.

#5: If you love craftsmanship and other delightful things, you'll have no issue identifying with a Libra sign. Attempting new things together, particularly if it's things like investigating nature, seeing craftsmanship displays, or accomplishing something imaginative together, can assist you with fashioning a bond with Libras.

Outline: Libra Traits

In case you're a Libra, you're following after some admirable people. Serena Williams and Will Smith, for instance, are exemplary Libra instances of adjusting hard working attitude, fun, and imagination. Libras can flourish much more when they know themselves and speak the truth about what their identity is and what they need. Ideally you'll have a superior thought of being a Libra, and figure out how to be the best form of what your identity is.

Libra Positive Traits

Sentimental

Librans go bonkers with regards to sentiment as they are administered by the planet of adoration, Venus. Everybody can get somewhat insane in affection, yet Librans are something other than what's expected than others. You are powerless against turning out to be totally love-tipsy.

Beguiling

It comes to Librans normally as they are brought into the world with all the appeal. Libra people are incredibly beguiling and a piece coquettish. Your amicable and enchanting nature makes you unimaginably alluring to other people.

Incredible Listener

You absorb all the thoughts and data around you like a major brainy wipe. You scorn clashes and encounters thus like to listen more often than not. You generally watch your words while conveying and for the most part talk such that nobody gets injured. Additionally, you tune in to everybody's side of the story before settling on choices so you can concoct reasonable choices.

Reasonable

Libra people are known for having intelligent personalities and a reasonable judgment. Librans make progress toward decency and equity continually. You generally energize reasonable arrangements and focus on what is being said. This makes you superb arbiters. You dissect each circumstance with your little legitimate bird cerebrum and sensible psyche. With the assistance of that you arrange everything great and wipe out insignificant things.

Visionary

You generally submit penny percent to everything. You generally need the best understanding. You will in general make impeccable manners all the time through your intelligent and judicious reasoning. You overthink in all circumstances and criticize the best out of it. Nonetheless, you additionally think about the individuals around you. You will get things done or settle on choices in a manner that is advantageous for all.

Understanding

Alongside being tasteful, friendly and energetic, Librans are likewise understanding. You are exceptionally insightful and decipher things that a great many people pass up.

Libra Negative Traits

Languid

"L" for Libra and furthermore "L" for Lazy. Truly, languid Librans are at times unfit, regardless of whether genuinely or intellectually, to finish a given activity. You like to do things that are simple.

Uncertain

Being an indication of scales, you are known to be somewhat hesitant. You struggle choosing what direction to go as you continually gauge the upsides and downsides of each choice.

Problematic

What makes you problematic is your few characters. You are now and again incapable to represent even yourselves so it is difficult for anybody to depend or rely on you to have their back in significant circumstances.

Shallow

Libra people are exceptionally shallow. You have a characteristic liking to visual magnificence as your decision planet is Venus.

Book: The Personality of a Libra, Explained - Author: Sikandar Sami

Manipulative

Libra people tend to control others. Since they can burrow profound and know the shortcomings of others, it is simple for them to control anybody and get them to do things they need. You make progress toward everything to be going great. You can oil all the difficulties and patch wall whenever required as you are a favorable to negotiator. In any case, all your compassion, tuning in, profound getting, suppositions, and wants will never be known. Now and again, you may not even truly know your own psyche.

Breaking down the places of planets right now of your introduction to the world will give you great understanding into your zodiac sign character attributes and will uncover the significance behind your sign. Get your Free Personalized Janampatri and get most profound experiences in your zodiac sign.

21 Secrets Of The Libra Personality

1. Libra will pardon... however they wont overlook.

The Libra doesn't have the opportunity to squander on holding superfluous feelings of resentment and when somebody botches they are typically sympathetic enough to allow them another opportunity.

Anyway they're additionally shrewd enough to gain from their missteps and they will in general remember everything so they don't make a similar blunder of judgment twice.

2. Libra regularly searches out longer-term and more significant connections.

Libra is hard-wired to search out longer-term and more important connections rather than shorter and additionally transitory excursions.

They're likewise ready to be patient and trust that the opportune individual will go along and wont simply agree to the primary individual that shows intrigue.

3. Libra is reasonable, adjusted and brisk to concede when they're off base.

The Libra is a solid backer of truth and equity and they will make a special effort to ensure that everyone gets reasonable treatment.

They're not reluctant to go to bat for those that who are dealt with ineffectively and they're additionally speedy to admit to their own errors instead of attempting to 'pass the fault' onto another person.

4. Libra is insane astute and incredibly 'turned on'.

Keep in mind the knowledge of a Libra for they have probably the most cunning and 'turned on' cerebrums in the entirety of the zodiac.

They are basic scholars who are more than equipped for introducing and shielding their thoughts with rationale and reason.

5. Libra doesn't think anything without seeing it with their own eyes first.

The Libra will in general be amazingly doubtful ordinarily deciding to dissect things unbiasedly and reach their own decisions... instead of depend on the tattle of others.

They like to see something with their own eyes before they trust it to be valid.

6. Libra is a smooth arbitrator who can convince individuals not to do moronic things.

At the point when individuals dismiss reason and a circumstance resembles it's going to break out into disarray... the Libra has a present for intervening and talking sense into individuals.

They can be exceptionally conciliatory and very enticing and can resolve a circumstance so that everybody feels fulfilled.

7. Libra is very perceptive and frequently knows more than they let on.

The Libra is continually watching their general surroundings and they are continually taking notes in their psyche about the things that they see.

They frequently get on things that others miss and they have an uncanny capacity to peruse a people musings and goals before they've even said a word.

Book: The Personality of a Libra, Explained - Author: Sikandar Sami

8. Libra can't stand narrow minded and rude individuals.

On the off chance that one's will undoubtedly exasperate Libra it's narrow minded and immaterial individuals that lone post for themselves while jaunting over every other person simultaneously.

In the event that you you're a self-important smarty pants type that won't tune in to what any other person needs to state then Libra will just block you out.

9. Libra has a chill and laid-back way to deal with life.

One of the Libra characteristics that they are maybe most notable for is their fairly chill and laid-back way to deal with life.

They make an effort not to get ended up over senseless things or dramatically overemphasize circumstances and they're ready to stay cool and reasonable in any event, during outrageous disorder.

10. Libra can be ludicrously enticing and difficult to state no to.

At the point when Libra talks they can at times appear to bode well... that they are practically difficult to state no to.

Their sound rationale and fantastic route with words permits them to get others to come around in their mind effortlessly!

11. Libra overlooks the haters and follows what they need.

Libra doesn't have the opportunity to lounge around the entire day tuning in to analysis from individuals who never really mope and whine.

Book: The Personality of a Libra, Explained - Author: Sikandar Sami

They are activity takers that accept that 'where there is a will there is a way' and with regards to their fantasies they follow what they need paying little mind to what anyone says.

12. Libra can be amazingly enchanting and somewhat of a tease.

At the point when Libra is truly burrowing somebody's vibe they can intuitively turn on the appeal and their well disposed and coquettish nature can make them extraordinarily alluring to other people.

They can be amazingly alluring without understanding that they are doing it... it just easily falls into place for them!

13. Libra is determined and continually thinking a couple of strides in front of their opposition.

Libras don't care to settle on inept and nonsensical choices spontaneously yet rather will in general be incredibly determined and prudent.

They're continually thinking a few strides in front of their opposition to ensure that the chances are constantly stacked in support of themselves.

14. Libra can't be with a darling that is egotistical.

Libra has a great deal of affection to provide for the opportune individual yet they can't be with someone who can't respond that adoration.

They need somebody who comprehends that connections are about 'give and take' and who can furnish Libra with the affection and empathy that they require from a relationship.

15. Libra would want to lose a contention than lose a fellowship.

Some zodiac signs can be so difficult and pigheaded in their inclination that they are happy to lose a completely decent fellowship over absolutely trivial and inept contention... however not the Libra.

On the off chance that something is simply not worth quarreling over and appears as though it could demolish a companionship then the Libra is eager to surrender and let them have their triumph.

16. Now and again Libra squeezes themself attempting to fulfill others.

Here and there Libras want to ensure that people around them are glad can prompt them squeezing themself to attempt to figure out how to satisfy everybody.

They need to recollect that they can't please totally everyone completely constantly and that it's alright once in a while to pay special mind to themself.

17. Libra is a great audience and they offer some executioner guidance as well.

Libra is the sort of companion that will drop everything to give a companion their ear when they need it.

What's more, not exclusively will they truly hear you out however they additionally offer some quite incredible guidance also on account of their sensible nature and capacity to see a circumstance from each side.

Book: The Personality of a Libra, Explained - Author: Sikandar Sami

18. Libra is receptive and interminably inquisitive.

The qualities and attributes of interest and liberality are very regular inside the Libra character and they are consistently on the chase to find novel thoughts.

They accept emphatically in not passing judgment superficially and want to prop a receptive outlook when up into new circumstances and meeting new individuals.

19. Libra is a social animal who aches for animating discussions.

The Libra will in general be very social essentially and they love to associate with others through intriguing and interesting discussions.

They are viewed as the "communicators" of the zodiac and there are hardly any things that they appreciate more than discovering somebody that they can simply become mixed up in discussion with.

20. Libra can be absolute erratic now and again.

Like the entirety of the Air signs the Libra can be very unusual now and again and exactly when you imagine that you have them all sussed out they will proceed to accomplish something that you never observed coming.

Their flighty and unconstrained attributes guarantee that life is never exhausting when Libra is near.

Book: The Personality of a Libra, Explained - Author: Sikandar Sami

21. Libra feels most joyful when everybody they love is upbeat.

Libra is about their loved ones and they feel at their absolute best when people around them are likewise feeling their best.

They will put forth an admirable attempt to guarantee that everybody that they love is glad in satisfied and it's consequently that they make for a damn decent individual to have in your life!

What planet is Libra managed by?

Individuals brought into the world under this sign are controlled by Venus, the planet of magnificence and love, which clarifies why they are so delicate and kind. Libra character's affection for workmanship, culture and excellence are down to Venus' impact. On account of Venus' impact, the seventh zodiac feels most calm when encircled by imagination.

Basic realities to think about this sign

We've chosen 15 realities about the Libra character that you should know!

Solid focuses: Equilibrium, equity, harmony

Characteristics: Curiosity, friendliness

Shortcomings: Doubt, triviality

Pearls: Sapphire, valuable coral

Hues: Pastels

Metals: Copper, platinum

Relating Body Parts: Kidneys, bladder, prostate

♎ Essential crystal gazing data: ♎

Cardinal sign Libra is an unobtrusive heavenly body that contains no stars of the primary extent, it ranges from 180° - 210° along in divine longitude. It was once viewed as the hooks of the Scorpion which is the reason its stars are named after it. In old style folklore, it was known as the sizes of Astraeus.

What fulfills these people?

For whatever length of time that things remain straightforward and evade confusions, Libra individuals are cheerful. They love living at the time and love investing significant energy to seek after their inventive diversions. Investing significant time for themselves among their bust timetable is significant for their and encourages you get away from all the madness.

A Gemini is the best counterpart for this zodiac sign. Together this pair will live a merry relationship on the grounds that their horoscope similarity is solid. This pair will never get exhausted and their optimistic and fantastic characters will guarantee they ricochet off of one another. These locals scorn strife, so they can't live with somebody they contend with throughout the day. The individual they had always wanted is propitiatory, cherishing, mindful to their necessities and in consistent pursuit of concordance.

What kind of individuals would it be advisable for them to evade in affection?

These locals must be careful about the individuals who utilize their buildings and absence of certainty against them. Egotistical individuals who feel better than others may wind up cutting them down and diminishing their sparkle. On the off chance that somebody helps them again and again to remember their deficiencies, they should disregard the possibility of a relationship.

Which Tarot card relates to Libra? It's Judgment

The Arcanum of Judgment, the twentieth card of the Tarot Marseille, delineates a winged figure playing the trumpet more than three characters ready to supplicate. It's the card of restoration, advancement and development, speaking to opportunity and the finish of a troublesome circumstance. The stop declares a great change, after a troublesome circumstance, which brings quietness and energy.

What is the importance of judgment in a Tarot spread?

- Positive viewpoints: Love from the outset sight, quality, probability of expert development.

- Negative viewpoints: Divorce, division, insecurity.

I don't get it's meaning to have Libra as your rising sign?

To have Libra ascending in your natal diagram causes you try to adjust and congruity. Accordingly you normally escape from tense or upsetting circumstances. For a few, this ascendant makes them grouchy and far fetched, though for other people, it makes them significantly more discretionary in their associations with others.

Your sun sign + Libra rising:	Main traits described:
Aries sun Libra rising	Loving and frank
Taurus sun Libra rising	Charming and sensual
Gemini sun Libra rising	Adaptable and successful
Cancer sun Libra rising	Romantic and attentive
Leo sun Libra rising	Fun and ambitious
Virgo sun Libra rising	Balanced and seductive
Libra sun Libra rising	Creative and romantic
Scorpio sun Libra rising	Sweet yet sour
Sagittarius sun Libra rising	Fast and hard working
Capricorn sun Libra rising	Emotional and detached
Aquarius sun Libra rising	Friendly and outgoing
Pisces sun Libra rising	Sexy and sweet

www.ingramcontent.com/pod-product-compliance
Lightning Source LLC
Chambersburg PA
CBHW060008230526
45472CB00008B/2005